PROFIT NOW!

Learn Valuable Strategies
You Can Start Using
RIGHT AWAY
to Increase Sales &
PROFITS!

JERRY LEVINSON

PROFIT NOW!

Published by:
Levinson Consulting Group
5Foot6Consulting.com
A Small Family-Owned Business
NO ONE OVER 5'6"

Book design by:
Hollister Design Group
Scottsdale, Arizona

ISBN: 978-0-9899203-1-5

My wife Meg helped me out tremendously with this book. She also helped me by keeping the kids at bay so I could write when I needed to. Speaking of the children, all great kids who proudly make up our Small Family-Owned Business (No One Over 5'6"). They make life fun and meaningful.

My son Shane just got out of the Army after four years and one tour in Iraq and one in Afghanistan. He's always shone himself to be a reliable man who takes care of himself. I'm proud of what he's done and I'm anxious to see what he does with his life. He makes being a Dad fun.

My first daughter, Mrs. Emily Rose is a blast. She's got a great personality with her own style for fashion. She attends marketing and business conferences with me and we enjoy watching Shark Tank together. She understands that you don't need a job to make it in this world. You can create your own business and do what you wish to do in life.

Sarah is my happy girl, full of energy and life. She really loves to laugh and this girl knows how to play.

Hannah is the hugger. Always said I should drop her off at an old folks home so she could go around and hug everyone. She's such a sweet kid.

We are raising them in hopes that they will do more than just get a good job but understand how business, investments, and money work. They also need to understand that it's okay to fail and it's okay to screw up. Life is understanding and forgiving and it will give you opportunities to be the best you can be.

Further dedications go to my good friend Jim MacMillan. He not only helps me with all of my marketing and projects he also as good friend as a person can ask for.

I'd also like to thank my Master Mind group. Trish McCarty, Edward Maznio, Zach Wilsterman, Rich Rose, Clint Johnson, Superman & Lois Lane (A.K.A. Joe & Janette Gleason). Our fearless leader, Chuck Trautman, is especially instrumental to me when I need advice, especially on tough decisions. I'm not sure how anyone can achieve greater things in life without great mentors and friends. The best place to find this is most certainly at a Master Mind. You can go to Arizona Marketing Association to meet Chuck Trautman and learn more.

And last but not least, I don't know how I would get this book done, edited, and published without Brandi Hollister. She designs my front and back cover and keeps me on track. If you need help with your book, send her an e-mail at brandi@hollisterdesigngroup.com.

CONTENTS

It was 2009 and I was working with a shutter company who bragged to me that they did the same amount of work this year as they did in the previous year. If you remember in 2009 many businesses had either filed bankruptcy or they were hurting really bad because the economy collapsed.

Never the less, this company was proud of the fact that they didn't really lose any business, in fact they produced slightly more shutters in 2010 vs. 2009. "Even though we made less money, at least we had the same amount of work or a little more." he said to me.

I wrote *Profit Now!* because I wanted to help entrepreneurs and business men and women understand that this scenario is not necessary. You are quite capable of earning more money in the same business you are in. Use the information, exercises and lessons in this book to grow your business, work less, and *PROFIT NOW!*

You are going to learn how to raise your prices, get the most out of your employees, make it easy for your customer to buy, market in a way that you will be attracting the best clients, leadership and management skills, and a whole lot more.

Let me be real clear. This book is written for people who wish to make more money, not people who want more work. Working harder for less money has become the American Way. I'm here to redefine the American Way.

The first step is yours to take. Reading this book will help you, but only if you value yourself, your time, your expertise, your family, and your quality of life. I want you to make more money then you ever have, and I want you to do it in a way that brings you great enjoyment and pride for the business you run. The more you earn the more you can pay your employees, the more employees you can have, the more you can give to church, or a friend in need. The more you earn the better you can serve your clients. You owe it to your customer to charge them the full market value you provide, so you can do the best job possible.

1

WHO'S IN CHARGE
AROUND HERE?

WHAT'S THE MOST IMPORTANT INGREDIENT
TO YOUR SUCCESS?

Ever watch one of those shows where they go to a struggling or failing business and help the business turn around? I'm talking about shows like *The Profit, Bar Rescue, Restaurant Impossible*, etc. The expert always comes in and points out problems with employees, products, processes, marketing, environment and business layout.

If you look at all these problems, they stem from one thing— poor leadership! You can fix a business' marketing, operations, and even help the employees perform better at their jobs, but unless you have a good, strong, positive leader at the helm, these fixes really won't make much of a difference.

This book is about PROFITS. It's not just about increasing sales. It's about putting more money in your pocket. In the following chapters I describe ways you can make more money. This chapter is a little different. I'm going to talk about the importance of leadership, because without leadership you will not only lose profits you're going to lose your business.

WHAT MAKES A LEADER GREAT?

A Great Leader Makes Decisions!

He will decide how to go forward without worrying about being right or wrong. A great leader understands he can adjust and that mistakes are learning experiences and opportunities to grow and change.

He follows his instincts and he will do things that his employees, friends, and family disagree with, mostly because they don't understand. He doesn't follow conventional wisdom because if you follow the crowd you won't be exceptional.

If you allow fear to prevent you from trying new things, such as new products or new advertising, you will be stuck in neutral and your company won't grow.

When Truett Cathy of Chick-Fil-A decided that they would not open their restaurants on Sundays he went against the advice of all the chain restaurants and he risked being able to open in the malls. How much money was Truett leaving on the table by being closed on one of the busiest days of the week, Sunday?

Due to this very difficult and controversial decision Chick-Fil-A has become one of the leading fast food restaurants in America. His employees love it that they don't have to work on Sundays. Franchise owners don't have to schedule people to work on Sundays. Everyone gets a day of rest, period. People flood that restaurant on Saturdays now because they know it will be closed on Sunday.

My kids even know that we are likely to go to Chick-Fil-A on Saturday because we won't be able to go on Sunday. It's odd to see them dark in a mall on Sunday when everyone else is busy. In fact it's so odd that it makes for excellent advertising. One of the first rules of advertising is to stand out and get noticed. You can hear people talking and saying, "Look at that,

I wonder if Chick-Fil-A went out of business?" Then someone else will explain how their business operates.

A Great Leader Doesn't Have to be the Smartest One In The Room

She understands what her strengths are and she seeks advice from those who are more knowledgable. In making her decisions she will decide whose plan the company follows. She will decide to do what is in the companies best interest even if the idea didn't come from her.

Success is a team effort and you need smart people on your team to help you grow your company. One of my favorite sayings comes from Loral Langemeier, "There is no such thing as a self-made millionaire, it takes a team."

We usually go to our family and friends for their opinions and advice. It's great, they are supportive of our ideas. In fact they are so supportive and nice that they will lie to you rather than risk hurting your feelings.

I've seen this many times when advertising. You show someone your ad and they usually will tell you they like it, when what you really need is honesty about your message and how you can make your ad better.

If you want to lead your company and team you need to ask the advice of experienced professionals, not family and friends. The best advice may hurt your feelings and your ego may take a hit, but smart candid advice can save you a lot of money and more important it can make you a lot of money.

The Power of a Master Mind

One of your greatest resources should be a Master Mind. Napoleon Hill, author of *Think and Grow Rich*, was a big believer in the power of a Master Mind.

Hill defines a Master Mind as a "coordination of knowledge

and effort, in a spirit of harmony, between two or more people, for the attainment of a definite purpose."

I've been a member of a Master Mind for more than three years now and I can tell you it's made a big difference in my success. In my current Master Mind there is an owner of a charter school, Trish McCarty, and her CFO, Rich Rose; and a financial advisor and his wife, Joe and Janette Gleason. Janette started her own business in our Master Mind using Infusion-Soft. She wrote a book called *Momprenuer*. These two have done remarkable things to grow their businesses and lives while in Master Mind. My friend Edward Maznio grew and sold his hearing aid business and he is know traveling the country in a motor home with his kids and maintaing a healthy income. He's living life long dreams and he's only in his 40s. Zach Wilsterman owns a machine shop and has grown his business with great marketing, leadership, and support from his Master Mind. He's also in another master mind with a group of machine shop owners, very powerful! Clint Johnson owns a dental insurance practice, he joined recently and he's making great strides, learning how to raise prices and run a more profitable business that doesn't take up all of his time. The leader of our group is Chuck Trautman. He owns Arizona Marketing Association and I would encourage you to look into this. *(You can e-mail me at jerry@5foot6consulting.com for more information.)* Chuck gave me great advice that helped me sell my window covering business and he and my mastermind group continue to be my greatest mentors.

The reason I mention who is in my Master Mind group is to show you how diverse the group is. We have retail businesses, an educational business, health related businesses, a financial advisor and more. You never know which member is going to provide you with great advice. It may be because of an experience that they had or it could be because they just attended a seminar or read a great book.

A Master Mind is not a networking group. You don't join it looking for leads and more business, you join it to get honest feedback on best practices in your business. Your looking for constructive criticism on how your marketing looks and how effective it may be. You will get help on how to handle issues of hiring and firing employees. You will also get help on issues such as, best customer practices, legal challenges, landlord issues, and even personal issues involving your marriage and family.

A great Master Mind can help improve every aspect of your business and personal life. Not only will you get tremendous advice and help, you will have the opportunity to help others. One of my favorite things about being in a Master Mind is being able to help others by sharing my experiences with them.

In your Master Mind you will also have an opportunity to spend time with your peers, the 5% of the people who are running businesses that truly move America and make it great. Entrepreneurs are often the most misunderstood people out there. In order to be successful you have to go against the 95% to do something different and special. You will be misunderstood by your family and your friends. The people who will get you the most are the crazy entrepreneurs sitting across the table from you in your Master Mind.

To sum up this section, in order to provide great leadership you need to reach out for help and advice from others who are smarter, and experienced in areas that will benefit you. Great leaders don't always have the answer, great leaders know where to find the answer.

A Great Leader Knows How to Get the Most Out of Employees

Their can be a real love hate relationship between employees and owners or bosses. There is no place where Leadership is more important than dealing with your employees. They crave good Leadership, they're starving for it.

I was watching an episode of *Restaurant Impossible*, and one of the waitresses, Cindy was talking about her boss. Now this was a nice guy who got along great with everyone who worked for him. But the way Cindy described her boss was, "Rick is a nice guy but no one has respect for him, he used to be an ass hole but at least I made money then!"

All the employees goofed off in this restaurant. They all liked Rick but they didn't respect him, therefore they didn't respect the restaurant, the customers, or their jobs. And even though the atmosphere was light and fun with no pressure all of the employees hated it.

When the restaurant was reformed and Rick understood he had to be a tougher leader, everything changed. The employees worked harder. They made a better conscious effort to serve their customers. The employees also made more money and the "not so strange" part about this: <u>they liked their jobs better!</u>

It's difficult for many small business owners to think of themselves as "The Boss." A lot of them are afraid their employees won't like them and they would rather be friends then some boss who they talked bad about, feared, and in some cases hated. For the health and success of your business you need to keep a boss/employee relationship. It will be good for your company and it will be good for your employees as well.

I run a family-owned business. I like the people who work for me, but I don't get involved in their personal lives. I don't friend them on Facebook and I'm not going on vacation with them. That doesn't mean we can't go out to dinner and in one case we made it a tradition to go out to the movies together. When the new Harry Potter movies were coming out I made it a point for us to take the day off and take the company to the movies.

We loved it, we talked about the movie and we used to talk about the books. You just want to be careful because some day you may have to fire that employee, or they may need to quit for a better opportunity so it's best to maintain a professional relationship.

The best way to handle your employees is to lay down proper expectations. You want to create goals and incentives to influence your employees to do a great job and exceed those expectations. A lot of small business owners look to keep costs down in regards to their employees, but the best way for you to *PROFIT NOW* is to find ways your employees can make even more money. For example, let's say you own a paint store. You might give your salesperson more money for reaching a goal or selling at a high margin or getting a high closing rate. For the girl who is answering the phones you can give her an incentive for calling back previous customers. An extra $25 for every appointment set with a previous customer will go a long way in making her very happy.

As the leader of the company it is your responsibility to set the culture of your company. You need to identify why it is you do what you do and get your employees on board with that. We'll discuss the importance of a weekly meeting in a future chapter. With weekly meetings you can help your employees get on board with your mission and you can create a culture for your company that is a driving force for success and yes, PROFITS!

You want to empower your employees to take care of your customers, and help drive the company to great success. I was asked by a client once, "Do you think if we pay Becky more that she would do a better job?" The answer, "NO." If you give Becky clear responsibilities and empower her to do more she will enjoy her job more and be more productive. People do not work for money. That may sound odd but I don't really know anyone that simply works for money. If they do chances are they are not doing a very good job.

I used to watch basketball with my son and he would comment about the guys on the bench, "How great that would be to make millions of dollars and you wouldn't have to do anything." The truth of the matter is those guys hate doing nothing. My son has also joined the army and he served in both Iraq and Afghanistan. The time he enjoyed his service the most was also the most difficult time, basic training. They worked his ass off and he enjoyed the pace and the challenge. After that experience much of the time his job was to hurry up and wait, or guard a post, or do some boring meaningless task. He made decent money for that age and he had no real expenses but the money meant little to him, he would rather be busy and do something meaningful.

Your employees are the same way. They want to be useful, they want to do meaningful things, they want to be appreciated, they need feedback from you, and they need a pat on the back once in a while. I had a hard time understanding that myself at one time. One of my employees was about 20 years older than me. I looked at her as an intelligent person who didn't require praise from someone 20 years younger than her. Boy was I wrong. A lot of small business owners don't realize how meaningful their praise is to their employees. They don't look at themselves that way. It's much like being a mom or dad. What you say to your kids is very important. You mean the world to them and you are more important to your kids than you may realize. It's the same with your employees.

A Great Leader is One Who is Always Looking to Learn and Improve

I've always been fascinated by the gurus that I follow, Dan Kennedy, Joe Polish, Dan Hardy, and many more who are always reading new books or attending seminars. They are always learning. These people have succeeded multiple times and they are making a crazy amount of money and yet they are addicted to learning and growing.

David D. Glass, former president and CEO of Wal-Mart said of Sam Walton, "There's never been a day in his life, since I've known him, that he didn't improve in some way."

The fact is the way we do business is changing at a faster pace then ever before and if you don't try to stay ahead of the curve, if you don't look to be the game changer yourself, you will be left in the dust much like Blockbuster. Blockbuster was the top company to go to for movie rentals and now they are all but out of business. Netflix came in and found a new way to deliver movies that appealed to many taking major market share, then Redbox came in with their unmanned machines to deliver the final blow to Blockbuster. Blockbuster was to slow to make a change and therefore they didn't survive.

I attend many conferences from Dan Kennedy to Loral Langemier, Joe Polish, and more and these people are always showing new ways to market your product or service. They are showing new and creative ways of delivering your product or service. They are showing new and creative ways for you to make money.

I've also noticed that the quality of a seminar has more to do with where you are at in your business, and your attitude, then it does the content of the speaker. If you are in a place in your business where you are ready to grow and learn, you are seeking out specific knowledge that you can use to grow your business then you will get great benefits out of the conference.

Earl Nightingale says, "One hour per day of study will put you at the top of your field within three years. Within five years you'll be a national authority. In seven years, you can be one of the best people in the world at what you do."

To Be a Great Leader You Need to Pay Attention to Your Competition and More

A great leader understands how he can best compete with people in his industry. He will look for ways to be exceptional in ways that others can't keep up. *Do you understand who your competition is? Do you think about ways you can deliver your product or service that is unique and different?*

One thing I used to love is when Hunter Douglas, my main supplier, would offer rebates that sucked. I could hear my competition whining about how bad the rebates were and that those specials would not motivate customers to buy now. It absolutely stifled my competition. I, on the other hand, saw this as my greatest opportunity to offer my customers exclusive rebates and specials that no one else had. These were offers I created so no one else had them. Sometimes I would offer a double-rebate or I would extend the rebate to products that Hunter Douglas didn't offer rebates on. I would let my customer know this is a special arrangement I made with Hunter Douglas and it was exclusive to me.

To be truly great you must really understand who your competition is. For instance when you are marketing your competition is the people who are marketing in the same magazine as you, or in the same home show as you, they may be in the same newspaper as you. In the case of the newspaper you are also competing against the news. *(I'll explain more in the marketing chapter.)*

Disney says their competition is, "Everyone." They realize that they are competing against everyone their customer will do business with that day. Customers will compare their experience with you against their experience going out to dinner, or getting new tires, or even going to the Quick-Mart.

You've done this haven't you? You talked to your spouse about how lousy the service was you got at the grocery store and you compared that to your waitress and the restaurant you went out to dinner to. Didn't you say to your spouse, "If the grocery store would operate more like this restaurant I would probably do all my shopping there." Grocery stores are one of the places you can see a lack of leadership the most.

A great leader will notice when a company operates professionally with excellence and he will implement some of those strategies in his own business. He will go as far as to take the manager or store owner of another company out to lunch to learn some of his business policies, then decide which he can use to improve his own business.

———— EXERCISE ————

What are three areas you need to improve on when it comes to leadership?

Can you change these areas?

Do you need help changing in these areas?

_____

_____

_____

_____

_____

_____

_____

_____

_____

_____

_____

_____

_____

_____

_____

_____

_____

_____

_____

_____

_____

_____

_____

_____

_____

_____

_____

_____

_____

_____

_____

_____

_____

_____

For more information about how you can PROFIT NOW! with Jerry Levinson, see page 63.

2

THE EASIEST & FASTEST WAY TO MAKE MORE MONEY

IT'S QUITE SIMPLE REALLY - JUST RAISE YOUR PRICES!

That's right, simply charge more for your products or services. Do you know that if you charge 10% more for your products or services you would have to lose 40% of your business just to break even.

Raise Prices 10% = If you lose 40% you will break even.

You know you won't lose 40%. In fact you won't lose any business and you might even gain business. Let's do a little math here and see what a simple increase in price does for your business.

Say you own a Landscape Maintenance company. You charge $150 a month to cut and mow your customers lawn. Now let's raise your prices by 10%, which would be $15. (I didn't even need a calculator for this exercise)

Right now you are doing work for 75 homeowners and by-in-large they love you. Your crew is doing an excellent job and your such a nice young man.

Before you made $11,250 per month.

Your labor costs are $6,000 per month.

Leaving you with a profit of $5,250 per month.

Now you've raised your prices by just 10% and, let's face it, who's really going to shop around to save 15 bucks? Especially when they are satisfied with your work and they like you, because your such a nice young man.

Now you are making $12,375 per month

Your costs are still $6,000 per month. That hasn't changed.

Now you have a profit of $6,375 which is an additional $1,125 you will put in your pocket every month. That's an extra $13,500 a year.

How would you spend an extra $13,500?

Let's do another exercise showing you how you can really earn more. (These are real numbers from when I owned Blind Devotion.)

On average we sold to about 25 customers a month. Our average ticket was $2250.

Here we have two companies, Blind Devotion and We Sell Blinds Cheap. Now, the We Sell Blinds Cheap guys just loved more business, more customers, and more work. Let me show you how much they loved working.

On Average we each had 40 opportunities a month – 40 customers who wanted to purchase window coverings.

Blind Devotion	We Sell Blinds Cheap
Closing rate 45%	Closing rate 90% (they rocked)
18 customers sold	36 customers sold
Retail price for 12 wood blinds $2250	Retail price for 12 wood blinds $1560
$1100 was our cost	$1100 was also their cost
$1050 Profit x 18 Customers	$460 Profit x 36 Customers
$18,900 Total Profit	$16,560 Total Profit

Blind Devotion made $2340 more than We Sell Blinds Cheap. What else happened? Blind Devotion also did half of the work. We only had to pay our installers to install in 18 houses instead of 36 houses. Blind Devotion also had fewer jobs which means fewer problems, less mistakes, better customer service, and more time spent building the business and hanging out with our kids.

"But I don't want to rip people off." Great! Then provide the work you promised for the price you promised. More people get ripped off from the cheap companies then they do from the real expensive ones. The cheaper companies fall behind with paying their suppliers and they are constantly stressed. They are trying to run a volume type business with two guys and a truck.

NEWS FLASH! YOU ARE NOT WAL-MART!

With a closing rate of just 45% you can imagine we lost a lot of jobs due to price. It was always due to price. The problem wasn't that we were too expensive. The real problem is that our competition is too cheap. I value my knowledge, experience, and expertise, therefore so do my customers.

If you want your customers to value what you do then you have to value what you do first.

——— EXERCISE ———

Use the rest of this page and the next to write down some of your prices and, right here and now, raise your prices. Go just a little bit past your comfort level. You can always give a discount or come down a little. In fact your customers will appreciate the savings.

Then calculate how much more money you will put in your pocket by raising your prices. If you want a real simple way to figure this out, just figure out your total sales for the last year. You should have this figure in your books. Let's say it was $375,000. If you raise your prices just 10% then you should earn an extra $37,500 without doing any more work.

OK, it's your turn so dig deep and stick to it. If you only read this chapter and do this exercise, you are going to put a whole lot more money in your pocket.

_____

_____

_____

_____

_____

_____

_____

_____

_____

Let's dispel some common myths you may have about raising your prices.

1) ***My customers are more savvy now then ever before. They know what the price should be.*** – That's just not true. You've been in your business for several years, but even if you haven't, let's say this is a new business that you started. You researched the competition to find out the going rate. You gathered a bunch of information about your industry and your competition. *Before you did that you didn't know, so why do you believe that since you now know that your customer does as well?*

2) ***My competition will kill us. Their prices are so much lower than ours, we just can't compete.*** – Quit trying to compete on price. *How do you think companies who are two times to three times the price survive?* They market their company and product better and they don't try to buy the business of their customers by giving it away. I see companies everywhere like Kinetico who charges $5,000 for a water softener system when others are selling a system for just $1200. *How can they do that? How can they justify that dramatic of a difference in price?* Well they've been doing that for over 20 years now, so the real question is, *"Why the hell are the other guys still only charging $1200?"*

3) ***I don't want to rip people off!*** – *(I love this one.)* I'm glad you don't want to rip off your customers, so you should give them the products and service that they paid for at the price that was agreed to. If you look at the people who are ripping customers off it's not the ones who are the most expensive, it's the ones who are the cheapest. You will find they are the ones who can't afford to take as good of their customer, because if something in the project goes wrong they can't afford their mistakes. They

are also the ones who aren't paid up on their suppliers. They are trying to get more business by charging less money and digging themselves into an even deeper hole.

Most of the excuses people use about not charging more money come from their own nervousness. Once you do raise your prices you will be kicking yourself for leaving so much money on the table in the past. Some of your customers will even tell you, "It's about time!"

──────── EXERCISE ────────

Use the following work sheet to sketch out some of your prices and bump them up 10% to 20%. Experiment for a couple months and see what your results are.

_____

_____

_____

_____

_____

_____

_____

_____

_____

_____

_____

_____

_____

_____

_____

_____

_____

_____

_____

_____

_____

_____

_____

_____

_____

_____

_____

_____

_____

_____

_____

_____

_____

_____

_____

_____

_____

For more information about how you can PROFIT NOW! with Jerry Levinson, see page 63.

3

QUIT DOING
$10/HR STUFF!

I was driving around with a friend one day and he seemed visibly frustrated and stressed to the max. He was fairly new in his business so he was doing everything himself. He would call his suppliers to find out when he would get his products. He would contact the customers to inform them of when their service would be done. He would schedule the installers to do the work. He would follow up on problems from a previous job. With all this, he was getting overwhelmed and angry at the lack of business he was receiving.

I said, "Let me show you something." I made a phone call to my office assistant, Dana. I asked her, "Would you check on the shutters for Mrs. Deon and Mrs. Franklin, also follow up with Tanya Rigler?" Then I asked her to do two other things. I hung up the phone and I explained to my friend, "I have just as many problems and challenges as you do, the difference is I have a Dana."

————— EXERCISE —————

WHAT IS YOUR TIME WORTH?

Take a few minutes and figure out what your time is worth. *What do you do for your company? Are you the main sales person? Do you handle the labor? Are you the doctor, plumber, lawyer, etc.* Use the space below to figure out your hourly rate.

_____

_____

_____

Now I want you to write down all the things you are doing that don't make you that hourly rate. For instance let's say you clean pools or clean carpets or you spray houses for pest control. Now let's say you figured out you can earn $55/hr. doing the work you enjoy doing. *When you aren't doing that work what are you doing?*

Are you doing the paperwork? Are you answering the phones? Are you placing orders? Checking on Inventory? Sweeping the floors?

_____

_____

_____

_____

_____

_____

_____

_____

_____

_____

_____

Write down all the things you are doing that you could hire out. Yes I realize that you do those things better than a $10/hr. person but if you are serious about making more money in your business, you have to learn to trust people to do things for you and your company. Besides, mistakes can be fixed. Your employees will learn from their mistakes, because you will teach them the right way to do things.

_____

_____

_____

_____

_____

_____

_____

_____

_____

_____

Now take a minute and write down things you are doing that you shouldn't be doing.

_____

_____

_____

_____

_____

_____

_____

_____

_____

_____

_____

_____

Now let's get some work done. Let's say you hired a $10/hr. secretary. Now you have someone, full-time to answer the phones, do paperwork, keep up with suppliers, keep up with your customers, book flights for you, check on shipping, keep track of your books and so on.

Whenever you hire someone, you want to get the most value out of her or him. Their job will be to free you up so you can earn the most you can for your company, but how else can you *PROFIT NOW* from your newest hires?

They can call back previous customers who you haven't done work for in a while, write Thank You cards to your customers, follow up with warranties, check with your customers to see if they have any friends who would like to do business with you… catch my drift?

What are all the things you would like to implement in your business that you don't have time to do?

_____

_____

_____

_____

_____

_____

_____

_____

_____

_____

_____

_____

_____

_____

_____

_____

_____

Ready to dig a little deeper?

I'm going to assume that's a, "Yes."

Have you recognized how valuable your time is yet? Do you realize how much more money you would be making if you did the most productive things in your business and you hired out the rest? So let's carry this exercise over to your home life as well.

How much time do you spend cleaning your house? What would it cost to hire someone to clean your house and how much money could you make in that time?

Do you mow your own lawn? How much would it cost you to hire someone and how much money could you make in the four to six hours a month it takes to take care of your lawn?

Do you clean and maintain your own pool? Do you wash your own laundry? Do you shop for your groceries?

I understand that you may enjoy cleaning your house or gardening. I'm not suggesting you give up things you enjoy doing, but in order to make more money you need to hire out the things that other people can do for you, especially when it cost you very little.

When you don't enjoy, or benefit from doing certain tasks such as calling customers to schedule appointments, or making warranty calls, hire out those tasks to other qualified employees. When you're the owner of the company and you set your daily to-do list with lots of busy work, it's likely you'll become distracted and neglect the more beneficial tasks you should be doing to grow your business. But, once you put a good workforce in place and assign the "$10/hr." tasks to the right employees, it's a "win-win." This allows you to get on with the more difficult tasks associated with growing your business and *PROFIT NOW!*

For more information about how you can PROFIT NOW! with Jerry Levinson, see page 63.

4

HOW DO YOU GET THE MOST VALUE OUT OF YOUR EMPLOYEES?

HOW AM I SUPPOSED TO TURN THESE EMPLOYEES INTO PROFITS?

More important, how can these guys help me PROFIT NOW?

I had one client ask me this question, "Jerry, if we paid Amy more do you think she would do a better job?" NO. "Don't people work for money? Aren't they motivated by higher pay?"

People usually work due to obligation. Money is a great reward but great workers work great because that's the way they are built. People can be motivated to work harder. One way to motivate them is by paying more or giving them a bonus but that is a temporary fix. It usually doesn't last that long.

YOU NEED A WEEKLY MEETING

The best way to motivate your employees to perform better is to have a weekly meeting. Once a week you should meet with your entire team to go over the companies performance as well as some other issues I'm going to share with you. If you do this I guarantee you that it will be the best way you can multiply your sales and your income.

The first thing you need to do is have a good two or four hour meeting with your entire team. You may want to take it off site or schedule it around a lunch, but you need several hours for this first meeting.

- **Step 1) Share your goals, your dreams, and your vision for your company.** Get everyone on board. Get them excited! Let them know where the company is at with sales and what your overall goal for the year is. Get them involved and challenging you to do even more.

- **Step 2) Know your company's mission statement.** If you don't have one then now's the time to work on one with your team. *What do you want your customers to say about you? What impression do you want to give? If your customer were to post a review about you what would you want that to say?* Now talk to your team about that.

- **Step 3) Review products.** In the window covering business we have so many different products to choose from with different features and benefits. We like to go over one product and stay on that product for two to four weeks.

- **Step 4) Invite vendors.** This is a great time to invite vendors in to discuss their product lines. You let them know they need to schedule their presentations. For instance, you only do that on Tuesdays between 9 and 10:30 a.m. and you will give them 30 minutes.

- **Step 5) What does the future look like for your company?** *Are you going to expand? Do you want to retire and have one of your employees take over? Would you like your entire team to take over the operations so you don't have to work as much?* Get their input on how they can help make that happen. Ask them, "Karen, How do you think we can increase sales?" They have ideas too so get those ideas out of them.

- **Step 6) Keep your meetings somewhat short.** Sixty to 90 minutes is sufficient. Try to handle things fast and efficiently so people pay attention and they can get back to work. Everyone loves a short meeting.

Your employees will be so excited to be a part of something bigger with much greater potential. They will love going to work even more. They will love increasing the sales and their performance. They will be thinking about how we can improve our business now because they know that you give a damn about what they think.

YOU'RE EVEN GETTING EXCITED ABOUT THIS AREN'T YOU?

Establish a quarterly or semi-annul meeting just like this one and watch your company explode.

Now this will also be a time where you establish a weekly meeting. Your weekly meeting is just as important as a doctors appointment, a customer's phone call, a potential estimate, etc. You need to take this dead serious and you need to demand that your employees do the same. This is where you are going to really grow this thing. You and your team are going to start spending more time working on your business instead of just in your business.

What you want to do in your weekly meeting is have a set criteria that you go over every week. You should prepare an agenda to go over, but in case you didn't have the time at least you would have a set agenda that you can fall back on.

Here's a list of subjects for you to discuss:

- *Marketing:* Make your employees aware of any ads you are putting out. Are there any specials you have going on right now? Talk about future ads you would like to run, or marketing ideas. Talk about Future holidays, anniversary's, seasonal changes, home shows, etc.

- *Sales:* How has the sales team been performing? What is the closing rate? How can you improve? Take a moment to do some training on sales strategies and closing techniques.

- *Office procedures and systems:* How can you improve the flow of paperwork from the initial contact to the Thank You card?

- *Problems and solutions:* Problems come up during the week. I recommend that you take care of the problem but make a note to bring it up during the meeting. Now let's discuss how to handle these problems in the future. Let's figure this out as a team. What systems will we create to avoid the problem or take care of the problem?

VERY IMPORTANT! This is not a bitch session. Meetings are not the place to whine and complain. It's okay to bring up problems within the staff—such as communication—but make it clear to everyone that this is a time to figure out how everyone can work best together.

As the leader, boss, manager, or owner of the company, be cautious about bringing up certain matters to individual employees during the meetings. If you need to talk about taking too many breaks, or the way they dress, or other matters of personal nature, it's best to do that one-on-one and not at your meetings.

I encourage you to share sales numbers with the entire team because that will motivate them to try harder and compete against each other. Give out bonuses or special recognition during your meetings as well.

Everything I just laid out here for you will motivate your employees, grow your business greatly and it won't cost you any more money.

———— EXERCISE ————

Write down four or five topics you want to go over in your weekly meetings.

_____

_____

_____

_____

_____

_____

_____

_____

_____

_____

_____

_____

_____

_____

_____

_____

_____

_____

_____

_____

_____

_____

_____

_____

_____

_____

_____

_____

_____

_____

_____

_____

_____

_____

_____

_____

_____

_____

_____

_____

_____

_____

For more information about how you can PROFIT NOW!
with Jerry Levinson, see page 63.

5

WHY AREN'T YOU CALLING YOUR CUSTOMERS BACK?

INCREASE YOUR CLOSING RATE STARTING NOW!

Good communication leads to satisfied customers and PROFITS!

I'm amazed at how many sales people will spend their time and share their expertise with a customer, yet they don't respect themselves enough to call the customer back to see if they want to buy.

We secret shopped our competition back in 2013 and I was shocked to see out of 10 companies not one called back to see if we wanted to go with the order. Of course I was also thrilled that not one person called back. This is a huge problem with a majority of sales people. They met the customer, they gave her a bid, and now they are so terrified of rejection that they won't call back. I can tell you if that is you then get over it. You need to call people back and give them the opportunity to do business with you.

I also had a fear of rejection. I hated bugging people, but what I learned is that they were grateful when I called. People are generally nice and respectful, especially after you gave them a free estimate or free information.

This will really open up your opportunities to close. If your prices are higher, your customer will say, "I'd like to do business with you but you are X-amount higher." This gives you an opportunity to either sell your price, build confidence or match the price.

When you call back the customer will also realize that your communication process is better. They will have more confidence that you are going to be more responsive to their calls which is important. I once hired an attorney just because he was fantastic about getting back to me. The price and his expertise didn't matter. I needed someone who would respond to my questions and he proved he would do that before I ever gave him a deposit.

Sometimes a customer will not answer the phone or respond with a message when you do call back. Thank God for the invention of the internet and text messaging. *(And Thank Dean Jackson for the 9-word email.)*

9-WORD E-MAIL STRATEGY

This strategy is simple, effective, and brilliant. When you need to connect with a customer who you've made a connection with just send them this simple 9-word e-mail.

In the subject line you are going to put, "Hi Frank," unless she doesn't like to be called Frank. You can use your prospects name. First names are better than saying, "Mrs. Jones" because you want to be personable over professional.

Subject: Hi Mary

Message: Are you still interested in shutters for your home?

Message: Are you still interested in buying a home in Glendale?

Message: Are you still interested in a water softner?

Message: Are you still interested in painting the living room?

Message: Are you still interested in having your kidney's removed? *(Okay maybe it wouldn't work in this case but you get the idea.)*

Sales people tend to try to sell this customer all over again. They will send a message like this:

Hi Mary. I was wondering if you are interested in getting those rain gutters we talked about. You know with the storms recently I'm sure those would really help keep your sidewalks looking nice. Also if you need me to come down in price we can do that and fall all over ourselves telling you how great we are and how wonderful it would be if you would just read our really lengthy e-mail that will just turn you off and you will end up deleting anyway because it's way to long and you don't want to be bothered reading this so not only will you not read this e-mail you won't respond with a yes, no, or maybe so.

All right, I'm guessing that even you did not read that e-mail did you? Your customer won't read it either and they won't respond. Your goal is to simply engage to start a dialogue.

Now let's say she's not responding to phone calls or e-mails. Shoot her a text. The same technique works great—a 9-word text. She will send a response and you can either get the order going, you can learn she used someone else, or you can answer any questions she may have.

WHAT IS THE BEST WAY TO COMMUNICATE WITH YOUR CUSTOMERS?

Answer: The way that they prefer. I had one customer who only answered to text messages. Here's how specific it was. I was at her door knocking... no answer. I rang the door bell... no answer. I called her on the phone... no answer. Then I sent her a text message... she came right to the door! And when she answered what do you think she said? *"How come you didn't knock?"* It was pretty funny.

Recently one of our installers got locked out of a customers house. He knocked, rang the bell, and called but got no answer. We sent her an e-mail and she came to the door in seconds.

Another customer will only answer to instant messages on Facebook.

It's great to have systems in place so you can run an efficient business, but you have to be accommodating to your customers preferred method of communication. There's no reason to be frustrated by it because, at the end of the day, it's actually kind of funny.

EXERCISE

Since this is the *PROFIT NOW!* book, I want you to send out at least ten, 9-word e-mails to customers you haven't closed. It doesn't take any time and there's no reason you can't do this.

For more information about how you can PROFIT NOW! with Jerry Levinson, see page 63.

6

PUCKER UP BABY
& GIVE US A
K.I.S.S.

Or just "Keep It Simple Stupid" or even better, "Keep It Super Simple." *(I don't really care for the word "Stupid")*

Another phrase I like to use is, "Make the buying process easy."

When you are giving someone an estimate, include all the bells and whistles that make your product better and give it all to them for one price. Or, if you are doing a project give your customer the price of the entire project.

I was working with a designer today who does $50,000 to $300,000 projects. She normally breaks out the prices into the projects and she breaks out her fee. What we discussed is giving her clients one price for the entire project.

"Okay, Mrs. Jones We are going to do the glass tile in your kitchen and trim it out with the pieces you selected. You are getting the oak cabinets in cherry wood stain. We are going to put the Dom Fame granite on top. We are changing out your stove and fridge to stainless steel. My guys are redoing the ceilings with recessed lighting. And, last but not least we are installing the retractable disco ball for those 70s parties you like to throw."

"The total cost for your project is $175,396. We can have everything done within two weeks." *(Just like in the movie* The Money Pit *but of course we aren't going to tell her that.)*

If she wants to save money or she wants a breakdown she will ask for it. In most cases the customer will say, "Okay, that's a better price than I thought. Does that include installation, tax and everything?"

"Yes, that's the bottom line price for your entire project."

When you go buy a car do they breakdown the cost of the air conditioner, radio, floor mats etc.? I know it's on the sticker but do your really care or are you looking at what that car cost for you to drive off the lot? The only reason they give the menu of prices is because some legislature somewhere thought that would make them more honest and ethical.

Which brings me to another point. Some people feel it's more honest and ethical to break down the entire project so the customer knows what she is getting. Look I encourage you to be an honest business person. The way you need to do that is by providing the customer with the products and services you agreed on for the price you agreed on and in the time frame you promised.

In the beginning of this chapter I talk about "making the buying process easy" for your customer. *If she is buying an area rug are you ripping her off by selling her a no slip mat to go underneath?* Of course not.

Give her what she needs, give her what she wants, and make it easy on her by giving her one price for the project.

I had a TV station selling me advertising one time, and they had a menu of everything broken out in detail.

Writing the script	$125
Editing	$75
Lighting	$50
Shooting the commercial	$275
Running 30 60-second spots	$60 ea.

Total $2325

I read this and thought, "I wrote the script and I edited it." I started picking it apart. Now you see, they are at $2325. They could have told me, "Jerry, we will shoot your commercial, edit it, put background music up, and so on. You are going to love this and I really think this will help you get quality clients. we're also going to run 30 spots within two weeks during *Oprah* and all it will cost is $2500."

They could have charged me more and gave me more perceived value. Not only that, they could now come back and give me a better deal since I'm a return customer and my commercial is already shot.

"Jerry, since you ran with us last month my boss authorized me to give you a little better deal this month. We can actually run 40 commercials for you for the same price as before."

I would have been thrilled at this offer and taken them up on it in a New York Minute. Here's the thing, they would have made me extremely happy and at the same time they would have increased their PROFITS.

The problem is they haven't read this book so they will keep doing things the old way because they believe "that's what the customer wants." I'm not sure why they believe that but I did talk to the salesperson and that's what she told me.

If you sell carpet, window coverings, or any product where there are multiple opportunities for you to package your deals, *do so* and make it easy for your customers to buy.

DON'T GIVE THEM TOO MANY CHOICES

One of the problems that people have is when they have to many choices. It makes it hard to make decisions. How often do you ask the kids where they want to go to dinner tonight? It's because we hate deciding. When you give a customer too many options you make it hard on her to make a decision.

In the window covering industry it was a lot easier when there were fewer choices, styles, colors, and control options. Even though your industry provides a lot of options you don't have to tell your customer about all the options. The best thing to do is to give the custome two choices based on what you believe will look the best or be in their best interest. If they don't like either choice then you can pull out more options. Believe me you will make it much easier for them to buy.

Do you know at Costco you usually get two choices? The real expensive one and the less expensive one. They did that on purpose because they know if they give their customers too many choices they may not buy.

I see the same thing at the carpet store we have our showroom in. They provide way too many choices for their customers. The customers walk around in a daze and they can't decide. It also makes the showroom more cluttered and less attractive.

Note: Whomever invented the paint deck should be shot! Do we really need 50 shades of white to choose from?

Another strategy is to offer things like free installation. How many people want to buy a new roof and install it themselves? I'm guessing almost none. Again you will want to give your prospect a price for the completed project not every aspect of your project.

The Room Store created a brilliant way to increase their sales. When you purchase a certain amount most companies give you a discount. So, say you purchase $2,500 worth of drywall work. We will give you a $500 discount. What the Room Store did was to say if you purchase at least $2500 worth of furniture we will give you an additional $500 worth of accessories for free. That strategy helps to increase their average ticket price. How many customers spend $600 in pursuit of an extra $500 worth of accessories?

Another strategy I love is from places like Kohl's. They offer 50% off your second purchase. So if you buy one belt you get the second one for half off. *Who wouldn't buy the second belt for half price?* Their prices are higher to start with and instead of discounting the first purchase they increase the sale by half, brilliant!

—————— EXERCISE ——————

How can you encourage your customers to buy more from you NOW? Use the following pages to create some unique opportunities for your customers to spend more money with you.

_____

_____

_____

_____

_____

_____

_____

_____

_____

_____

_____

_____

_____

_____

_____

_____

_____

_____

_____

_____

_____

_____

_____

_____

_____

_____

_____

_____

_____

_____

_____

*For more information about how you can PROFIT NOW!
with Jerry Levinson, see page 63.*

7

SELL THEM
SOMETHING ELSE

WHO IS YOUR BEST CUSTOMER?

Who would be the easiest person for you to sell your products or services to?

Answer: The person who has already done business with you. They've already demonstrated that they like and trust you so wouldn't it make sense to try to sell to them again? That is the low hanging fruit.

Do you know that it costs nearly seven times as much to acquire a new customer than it does for you to go after an existing customer? And yet so many companies have great marketing expense and plans to get new customers.

One of the best things you can do to increase sales and *PROFIT NOW* is to contact your existing customers at least once-a-year. Depending on your industry you might step that up to two, three or even four times-a-year. In fact there are companies who send out a monthly newsletter.

Here are some great ways for you to stay in touch with your existing customer base.

1. **Send out a monthly newsletter.** A monthly newsletter is a fantastic way to stay in touch and stay top of mind to your customers. There are a lot of people who send out an electronic newsletter. Even though the cost is very little so is the effectiveness. Mailing out a hard copy is expensive and it's so much more effective. People will read your newsletter. They will keep it around and they will share it with friends. Your newsletter should be a combination of entertainment and great information. You can have humor, an article that your dog writes and seasonal tips. A puzzle like Sudoku works well to keep your newsletter around. You can also hire a company to put the newsletter together for you with clever articles, jokes, and games. That way it doesn't take you long to produce and send out to your customers.

2. **My favorite method is the "customer call back."** I recommend you hire a stay-at-home mom or get your sales people to do this. Call your customers back with a simple message:

   > "Hi Debbie this is Joan from Stay Right carpets. I'm calling you to see how your carpets are holding up for you. (She says they are fabulous) Okay, great! I also wanted to let you know that we are closing out some tiles right now so I have some incredible deals on tile, and we have great specials on our wood flooring too. I'm going send you more information in the mail.

   What we want to do is create a simple offer to connect and follow up with a letter. This one - two punch is very effective at getting more business.

3) **If you have e-mail addresses, send them an e-mail every month.** If you don't have e-mail addresses then you better step it up and start getting every person's

e-mail address. One thing that helps a nervous secretary is to tell her "either get the customers e-mail address or under ware size, which ever you feel most comfortable getting."

Now when you send out the e-mails it's very important to not be pitchy. You don't want to send offers and solicit. Be entertaining and interesting. *Who gets paid more, an entertainer or a teacher?* You want to send a funny story that may be relevant. You can talk about something interesting you found in the attic when replacing an air conditioner. You can show a scary bizarre paint job that may be a before picture before you start painting. Pictures of bad workmanship do more to sell good workmanship than good photos will. Everyone loves a train wreck.

4) **Use the good ol' US Mail.** That's right, just send them a letter or a post card. You can wish them a happy birthday, you can send them an anniversary card of when they got married or when they purchased something from you like furniture or wind chimes. You can send out a card for the holidays, but try to choose a more unique holiday than Christmas. Everyone sends out Christmas cards so it's difficult for you to stand out. You can send out a card for Thanksgiving, 4th of July, Valentine's Day, or one of my favorites, Pie Day, which is on March 14 (or 3/14). I have a friend who is an engineer and he always celebrates Pie Day by sending out a pie to his clients.

In the blind business many business owners say, "I'm not going to call my customers back because I'm afraid something will be broken." They are so afraid of problems, but here's what happens. If a customer has a problem with something they buy from you, they may decide to never do business with you again because your product stinks. And not only that, they are going to tell all their friends and family not to do business with you. The funny thing is they are mad at you and they didn't even tell you there was a problem. But if you are calling them once-a-year and you find out about the problem and take care of it, they are your customer for life. In fact those customers will refer you more than the customer who never has a problem.

——— EXERCISE ———

Use the next page to come up with just one action plan to reengage with your previous customers.

_____

_____

_____

_____

_____

_____

_____

_____

_____

_____

_____

_____

_____

_____

_____

_____

_____

_____

HERE ARE SOME OTHER GREAT WAYS YOU CAN PROFIT NOW!

Find something else to sell to your same market. If you sell swimming pools you can sell the same customers BBQ islands. If you sell carpet and tile you can sell the same customers window coverings. If you sell drugs you can sell the same customers Girl Scout cookies. *(Of course that is limited to only a few states at this time—and I am kidding—but you get the point.)*

Again you've already done the hard part, you got the customer. *How great is it for them to be able to buy something else from someone they like and trust?*

Sometimes it can be complicated to pick up another product line. There is a learning curve and you can take your focus off what you do best, so there is another way for you to sell something else to the same customer. Get an affiliate partner.

In 2009 the recession was taking it's toll on me and I had to move out of the small building I was in. I was paying $3 K a month for 1000 sq. ft. I met a guy who sold carpet and tile and I talked to him about moving into his showroom. I said, "Karl, *(I called him Karl, well, because that was his name)* ... Karl, why don't you and I team up? We can share the rent, advertising, and most all of our customers." This allowed me to keep a showroom and Karl and I were able to take advantage of the additional traffic each of us provided.

You don't have to move in with someone to become an affiliate. You can use each others list. You can either send out an e-mail on behalf of your affiliate partner, where you get a cut of the action or you can exchange your customers e-mail addresses. When companies do this they usually trade equal size list. So if I have 3,000 names and you have 12,000 then we may agree to just trade 3,000 names so it's equal and fair.

Anything you can do to touch a customer again and again and keep your company top of mind will build a solid foundation which will help you grow and *PROFIT NOW!*

———— EXERCISE ————

Choose at least three new products that you could sell to your existing customer base. Then choose how you will do that. *Will you sell it directly yourself or will you get an affiliate partner?*

_____

_____

_____

_____

_____

_____

_____

_____

_____

_____

_____

_____

_____

_____

_____

_____

_____

For more information about how you can PROFIT NOW! with Jerry Levinson, see page 63.

8

"I CAN HELP
ANYONE WITH A SPINE"

From a Chiropractor at a Networking Group

(REAL CUTE AND VERY INEFFECTIVE.)
CHOOSE A TARGET AUDIENCE.

If you look at Joe Polish's *9 Profit Activators* you will see the first one is to choose a target audience. Yes, I understand that you are capable of serving a wide variety of people. Choosing a target audience is one of the smartest strategies you can use to command higher prices and create the most effective marketing. When you choose a target audience you are not doing it to exclude others.

I was in a networking group where the Chiropractor used to say, "I can help anyone with a spine." Everyone used to laugh and then they would think of no one in particular because everyone we know has a spine, with exception to that one politician we had in our group but we won't get into that right now.

In another group there was a chiropractor who said, "I'm an expert at helping women golfers." Now anyone who knew a woman golfer or any of the women who golf had someone come to mind. This chiropractor is extremely successful targeting this particular audience. She charges more money and she's busier than most chiropractors. She's able to sell her service easier by describing who she serves rather than giving her credentials or telling people what she does.

There is a weight loss expert named Howie who told us a story about his sister. She said, "Howie, I'm driving the kids to and from school in my mini-van, I have to take care of the house and go to work, I have a stack of clothes in my closet that I want to fit into again, but I only have 15 minutes-a-day to work out. What can you do for me?" Howie has sold more weight loss programs with that story because the busy moms that he serves relate to the story. He's shown that he can help women like this lose weight. He made a connection without telling them anything about his technique. They like Howie because he understands them.

If you are a carpet cleaner you might want to specialize in cleaning carpets for people who suffer from allergies. You can advertise that your process is especially good for allergy sufferers. Again you can command more money because your service will be helping a specific demographic with a specific need. Now it's not about just cleaning the carpets, it's about curing their allergy problem. Oh and the bonus is I get my carpets cleaned to.

——— **EXERCISE** ———

***What you do has more to do with, WHO YOU SERVE.
Describe your best customer here.***

Is he a man or is she a woman? _____

What age? (Within 5 years)_____

Married or Single? _____

Widowed? _____

Kids? No kids? Empty nester? _____

Own a home or Rent? _____

Income? _____

Are they self-employed? _____

What kind of car would they drive? _____

Do they have pets? What kind? _____

Do they take vacations? _____

Do they own multiple homes? _____

Do they have allergies? _____

Special Interests? _____

Sports? _____

Do they golf? _____

Do they fish or hunt? _____

Do they Fornicate in the woods? *(Okay, that may be getting a little to deep.)*

Do they like to laugh? *(I'm kind of hoping you do.)* _____

Write down one or two descriptions of your perfect client.

_____

_____

_____

_____

_____

_____

_____

_____

_____

_____

_____

_____

_____

There isn't a single business that can't do this. When I owned the blind business I had several niches that I target advertised to. Here are some:

- Canadians
- Seniors
- Professional single women
- Gay couples
- Multiple home owners (or Snowbirds)
- Left-handed people *(This was a bit of a joke but it got a good response. We offered people left handed blinds. People who were left handed took notice because the ad was about them.)*

I'm not saying you should call out the specific details of your prospects lives when you are advertising. For instance I wouldn't say, "professional single women," but I did get a mailing list for them and I advertised the brand name and I promoted that, "We are a Small Family-Owned Business (NO ONE OVER 5'6")." This did a couple things. Professional single women are very busy and they won't get multiple estimates. Their biggest concern is to do business with someone they like and trust. Our family photo with the smart-aleck saying helps with like-ability. Brand name products like Hunter Douglas also build trust, and women prefer brand name items.

One time I advertised in the newspaper in a senior section, "50% off blinds for new home owners." I kept getting seniors in trailer parks, and they were wanting verticals. So I made the offer bolder and better, "New Home Owner Special SAVE 50%!" I still kept getting seniors buying verticals. Funny thing I noticed after awhile. There money went into my bank account just fine. Okay, let's try this one, "Senior Special, Save 75% on Vertical Blinds." Ka Boom! We just exploded with more business.

So if you sell roofing could you target specific neighborhoods based on the age of the home?

If you are a financial advisor could you target widows? Studies show that a woman who loses her husband will change financial advisors within two years after her husbands death.

There's a company who purchases used golf carts from widows and refurbishes them and sells them. They get the golf carts dirt cheap and sometimes they are getting them for free. The wife just wants to get rid of it.

If you are a pest control company could you specialize in households with kids because you have a very environmental spray that won't harm the children.

Everyone can specialize in helping specific people. If you do that you will stay busier and you will be able to command higher and higher prices which will help you to *PROFIT NOW!*

For more information about how you can PROFIT NOW! with Jerry Levinson, see page 63.

9

DO YOU HAVE
ANY FRIENDS?

REFERRAL MARKETING

Your next cheapest way to build your business fast.

If you ask most business owners what percentage of your business comes from referrals they would probably guess around 70%, without really knowing. It probably is closer to 50% in most cases. I know we were at 57% combined referrals and repeat business. If you ask why they get referrals, they will claim that it's due to their performance and customer satisfaction.

The problem is most business owners hope to get referral business. They hope their customers share their good fortune of meeting you. Hope is not a very good strategy. Most businesses don't have a referral plan or system to get that extra business from their satisfied customers.

Do you want to know the #1 system used for generating great referrals? Okay, I can see you nodding your head so I will reveal the #1 secret to generating quality referrals.

ASK for them! It may not be as simple as just asking for the referrals, though. You should create a system so you are asking for them at the best time. Some say that's after you make the sale; that's when their emotions are highest. Others will tell you that it's after delivery of the product or service. If you are disciplined about asking for referrals it really doesn't matter when you do it because it becomes a habit for you to do that.

One great reason for systematizing the referral request is that your salespeople and/or receptionists will ask when they're supposed to. Creating a clear referral system is a great way to ensure that everyone is doing that job properly and it will help you stay accountable for asking for referrals as well.

We always sent a check out to our customers offering a discount on their next purchase of window coverings. And if they didn't need anything at that time, to please pass the check along to a friend or family member. That worked well at getting additional business from either the customer or their friends. It's like Staples giving you money to spend in their store. It's hard not to take advantage of that. They know you are going to buy more when you are there.

REFERRAL GUARANTEE

I also offer a Referral Guarantee, which no one else does that I'm aware of.

> If you refer a friend to Blind Devotion we promise they will be satisfied with our service. If for any reason they are dissatisfied and they get upset with you we will replace them with a new friend at no extra charge. *(Family is not included in this offer, you are stuck with them.)*

Okay, if you can't tell by now I'm a bit of a smart aleck. But I did send this offer out to our customers and I advertised it on the radio. It's something that is funny and they talk about it which helps bring us up in the conversation. You're welcome to use that if you are so inclined.

PAYING FOR REFERRALS

I don't know the effectiveness of paying for referrals over simply asking for them. Customers who refer your business do it as a favor to their friends, they aren't referring you to benefit you. It's just like when you recommend a movie to a friend. You don't care how the box office does or how much money the theater makes. You recommend the movie because you know your friend will like it. Your customers will recommend you because they know you will take care of their friends. The monetary gain is nice but it doesn't have as big an impact on people referring as you may believe.

The best thing about offering a gift for the referral is that you have created a system. It's not the money that will help, it's the system that will work.

Okay, this should be an easy exercise for you.

———— EXERCISE ————

Create the system for asking for referrals that you can start using tomorrow so you will PROFIT NOW!

_____

_____

_____

_____

_____

_____

_____

_____

_____

_____

_____

_____

_____

_____

_____

_____

_____

_____

_____

_____

_____

_____

_____

_____

_____

_____

_____

_____

_____

_____

_____

_____

_____

_____

For more information about how you can PROFIT NOW! with Jerry Levinson, see page 63.

10

IMPORTANT KEYS TO SUCCESS ALL BUSINESS OWNERS SHOULD PRACTICE!

HOW I TOOK BLIND DEVOTION FROM A 1/2 MILLION DOLLAR-A-YEAR COMPANY TO A 1 MILLION DOLLAR-A-YEAR COMPANY

When writing this book I found it necessary to include this information even though it's not really *"PROFIT NOW"* advice. Anything that you build requires a good foundation whether it's a statue, a building, a family, or a business.

How to Have the Right Attitude

I noticed every book I've ever read and every guru I've ever studied had these two pieces of advice. The first one is to be grateful. You may not have as much as you want, which is good, that means you have goals which motivated you to try harder, but you have more today than you did last year.

PRACTICE GRATITUDE

Even if you went through a bankruptcy, or you lost your money, or you are going through some tough times, you have more knowledge and ability to make more money and become wealthier and happier. You do have a lot of things around you to be grateful for. You just have to focus on the things in your life that make you happy. You can be grateful for your family and friends. You can be grateful for your business, your job, or even your opportunities and future. You can certainly be grateful for your faith and things that have very deep meaning to you. Gratitude is one of the key essentials to happiness and without gratitude you will never become successful. Success is not defined in numbers. Success is defined as the happiness you experience from your achievements. *(Of course, this is the Jerry Webster's definition.)*

YOU NEED TO GO ON A VERY SPECIFIC DIET & EXERCISE PROGRAM

The second piece of advice is to exercise your brain. I'm not really a health and fitness kind of guy so you won't being getting advice on eating habits from me. I'm talking about a different kind of a diet. *If you do want to feel better, you will lose weight and exercise, right?* If you want to feel better, stronger, and more confident mentally then you need to exercise your brain.

The first step to a healthy brain is to go on a news diet. That's right – cut out the news. It's depressing to hear about all the murders, crimes, incompetent politicians, Middle East conflicts, and a whole host of other negative things. Knowing what's going on will not add value to your life. I'm actually a political junkie and I enjoy listening to talk radio but when I want to dig in and grow my business, I'll go on a news diet.

Now for the exercise. You need to build up that brain muscle of yours and whip it into shape. Read books like this one. Read a little bit about business every day. You can read blogs, newsletters, magazines such as *Success*, or daily advice from guys like Dan Kennedy from GKIC Marketing. When you are in the car you can listen to CDs like *Magnetic Marketing* or *Success* CDs or check out Joe Polish's *Piranha Marketing* CDs (you can pick up from Nightingale Conant). You can pick up

CDs from Brian Tracy, Jim Rohn, Tony Robbins and more just like them. Google is your friend.

If you are listening in your car you will get so many ideas that you can put into action… which brings me to my next point.

Become A Student

Become a student of business, marketing, sales, and money. Read more books about business advice. Order *Success Magazine*, which comes with a CD every month. Go to seminars and conferences about marketing and success. Join a Master Mind Group.

Hire A Coach

The greatest athletes like, Tiger Woods, Lebron James, and Payton Manning couldn't achieve the level of success they enjoy without good coaches. A great coach will get the best out of you. You need to find a coach who speaks to you. One you understand and who you enjoy listening to. I've hired coaches who thought they were psychologists rather than coaches. When I coach clients I give clear actionable direction that they can use to start making more money.

If you truly want to grow your business and you are willing to make changes, I would love to work with you. My clients learn how to work smarter. My goal is to help my clients reach their goals a lot faster. We do that with better lead-generating techniques, better sales systems, and better use of your team.

Set Goals

Have you set goals for yourself? If so that's great! If not well then it's time you get to it. You should have annual goals, as well as monthly goals. Some of the more successful people break it down to weekly and even daily goals. *How do you know if you've achieved success unless you have a finish line?*

One reason setting goals works so well is because you are making a conscious effort to grow your business and achieve success. After setting your goals, your brain will start working on achieving those goals automatically.

The purpose of this book is so you can *PROFIT NOW!* The tips in this chapter are for your long-term future and success. I'm rooting for you to succeed and have a wealthier, happier life.

To Your Success,
Jerry Levinson

Are You Ready To
PROFIT NOW?

Are you tired of...

- Being a stressed out business owner who is worried about making payroll, covering expenses, and trying to keep the doors open?

- Losing jobs to your competition or having to constantly cut your margins?

Jerry Levinson the author of Profit Now has worked with many business owners to help them increase <u>Profits Quickly</u>. With a few simple strategies you too can start enjoying more money in your pocket and more time with your family.

SEE WHAT BUSINESS OWNERS HAVE TO SAY...

I'm finally reaching my goals thanks to Jerry's system. I've taken a lot of what Jerry has taught me to heart and have started to reach my goals. I've raised my prices and I've learned how to leverage my employee's skills which makes my job so much easier as a business owner. And yes I do appreciate myself more!

Nancy S.
M&M Accounting

I'm running full speed ahead and have to thank you for giving me a new spark in my business.

I am very excited about my future in my business. It's a breath of fresh air to actually know and receive personal coaching from a business owner who made millions, sold their company and now ready to take on another business because of your zeal for marketing and business.

I've already shared with a few business owners about you and your advice, even some of my regular clients. They all agree I'm worth MORE and happy that I've met with you.

Davonna M. Willis, MA, ATC
Blue Skye's Massage Clinic

Sign Up For *Profit Now Coaching*
with Jerry Levinson

- Send an eMail to Jerry@5foot6consulting.com
- Include *I'm Ready To Profit Now* in the subject line

Jerry will contact you to schedule a free 20 minute discovery meeting

JERRY LEVINSON

I was born and raised in Phoenix, AZ. When I was a kid, I stepped on the lawn of a witch in our neighborhood and she put a curse on me. She said I would always live in Arizona, and I could only move in August. *(That's a little secret I kept from my wife until she married me.)*

I'm one of six boys in our family. My older brothers and younger brothers are twins and not anything alike in looks or personalities. My childhood was excellent and my goal in life is to give my kids the kind of childhood that my parents gave us.

I love life, I love business, and I'm fortunate to have achieved my goals of creating a well-run, profitable business, Blind Devotion, and sell it. My bigger goal was to provide consulting, which I am now doing full time and loving it.

This is supposed to be about the author and not a solicitation but the truth is I do love working with people to help them get the most out of their marketing, employees, sales process, and business as a whole. I am doing what I love so it's hard to call it work.

Life is full of fantastic opportunities. I hope you are working towards the goals that make you feel great to wake up every day, and even better when you are working until 1 a.m.

Made in the USA
Lexington, KY
25 April 2019